Grandmothers at Work

Meet My Grandmother

She's a Supreme Court Justice

By Lisa Tucker McElroy
(with help from
Courtney O'Connor)
Photographs by Joel Benjamin

THE MILLBROOK PRESS
BROOKFIELD, CONNECTICUT

For my grandmother, Zipporah Gross Hoffer, a retired teacher.

ACKNOWLEDGMENTS

Scott and Joanie O'Connor; Maggie Dupree, Linda Neary, Tim Moore, Carolyn Sand, Oona Hathaway, Traci Jones, Sandra Glover, Michael Scodro, and Matt Stowe in Justice O'Connor's chambers; Jeff Banaszak, a police officer at the Supreme Court; Kathleen Landin Arberg and Edward L. Turner, Jr., Supreme Court public information officers; Bill Moran, photographic assistant; Bryan and Rikk, managers of the Capitol Hill Guest House; Evelyn Riley, Janet Bunting, and Jackie Grattan, secretaries extraordinaire; the Rehnquist family; the Palmer & Dodge Literary Agency; Crispin's Bears, Andover, Massachusetts, and Lori Magno, who helped make the Justice bear; Mary-Rose Papandrea, former law clerk to Justice David Souter; everyone at Gadsby & Hannah LLP, especially Bill Zucker, Paul Clifford, and Evan Slavitt; Karen Copenhaver; Laura Hoffman and David Colin, for being so generous with their time and their home while I was in Washington; Patricia Wellenkamp and Anne Reagan Harris, for helping with the legal research; Bob's Famous Ice Cream, Bethesda, Maryland; Elizabeth Matthews and the staff of Barnes & Noble, Bethesda, Maryland; Child's Play, Bethesda, Maryland; Susan Cooper, Laura Diachenko, and the rest of the staff of the National Archives; Amy Dyson and the staff of the Air and Space Museum; Deanna Chambers and the students of the Sandra Day O'Connor High School, Helotes, Texas; Dr. Todd Shapiro; Dan Norman; and the McElroy and Tucker families; and my wonderful husband, Stephen McElroy. All photographs by Joel Benjamin except p. 7, Sandra Day O'Connor and p. 12 © Michael Evans/Sygma .

Library of Congress Cataloging-in-Publication Data
McElroy, Lisa Tucker.
Meet my grandmother: she's a Supreme Court justice / by Lisa Tucker McElroy
(with help from Courtney O'Connor); photographs by Joel Benjamin.
p. cm. — (Grandmothers at work)
ISBN 0-7613-1566-7 (lib. bdg.)   ISBN 0-7613-1386-9 (pbk.)
1. O'Connor, Sandra Day, 1930-   —Juvenile literature. 2. Women judges—United States—
Biography—Juvenile literature. 3. United States. Supreme Court—Biography—
Juvenile literature. I. O'Connor, Courtney. II. Benjamin, Joel. III. Title. IV. Series
KF8745.025M385 1999
347.73'2634—dc21
[B] 99-31130 CIP

Published by The Millbrook Press, Inc.
2 Old New Milford Road, Brookfield, Connecticut 06804
Visit us at our Web site: http//www.millbrookpress.com

I don't know which

is my favorite thing to do when I visit my grandparents—go bowling with my grandfather or hang out at my grandmother's office. Last November my mom and I went to Washington, D.C., to visit my grandparents, and I spent lots of time learning about what Grandma does. My name is Courtney O'Connor, and I'm nine years old. My grandmother, Sandra Day O'Connor, is an Associate Justice of the United States Supreme Court.

★

This is the building where Grandma works, the Supreme Court of the United States of America.

If you stand at the top of the steps and look out, you can see over to the Capitol building.

Grandma works in the **Supreme Court building** on Capitol Hill right in the center of Washington. It's a big marble building with forty-four steps from the street up across the plaza and up to the main entrance.

·EQUAL·JUSTICE·UNDER·LAW·

Across the top of the Supreme Court building it says: "Equal Justice Under Law." I asked Grandma what that meant. She explained that the job of the Supreme Court is to make sure that two things happen: that all people coming to the Court get justice and that the laws are interpreted and enforced fairly. That's why she's called a Justice. Including Grandma, there are nine Justices on the Supreme Court.

While Grandma and I were walking

into the Supreme Court, Chief Justice Rehnquist came up and said hi. He is the head of the whole Supreme Court. His granddaughter, Dana, was visiting him for the weekend, too. One thing that's neat is that he and my grandma were in the same class in law school and have been friends for many years, even before they were on the Supreme Court.

Grandma told me she never imagined that she would ever be on the Supreme Court.

When she and Grandpa were newly married, he was drafted into the Army and was sent for training in Virginia, right near Washington, D.C. One day, Grandma said, "Let's go see the Supreme Court!" And they did. The Court was closed because it was a Saturday, so they couldn't go inside, but they stood in front of the steps, and Grandma took Grandpa's picture. Grandma says that that was the closest she thought she would ever get to the Supreme Court.

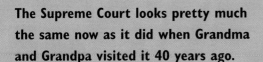

The Supreme Court looks pretty much the same now as it did when Grandma and Grandpa visited it 40 years ago.

Grandma says that all judges
who are grandmothers should start
their days by exercising.

In fact, everyone should! On the top floor of the
Supreme Court, there is a gym. My grandma organizes
aerobics classes on the basketball court there three times a
week. The basketball court is called "the Highest Court in
the Land." That's a pretty funny joke, because the Supreme
Court is also called the Highest Court in the Land. My
mom and I got to do aerobics, too.

It made me feel really good all day!

I think I was a little out of step
when this picture was taken!

After she finishes exercising, Grandma starts work. All nine of the Justices have offices called "chambers" in the Supreme Court building. Each Justice has helpers, called clerks, who have offices there, too.

Grandma's chambers look out over the Capitol building, where Congress meets. Her office is decorated with beautiful things from Arizona Native American tribes. She has drums and baskets and pottery. She says that her art reminds her of growing up in Arizona.

The basket on the wall is an Apache basket and I am beating on a Zuni drum.

Grandma uses this chair to keep her back straight so it doesn't hurt.

Before she was a Supreme Court Justice,

Grandma was a lawyer, a state senator, and a judge. She was such a good judge that, in 1981, President Reagan asked her to become a Justice. The day she was sworn in was an exciting day for America, because she was the first woman Justice in the history of our country. I'm not in the picture because I wasn't even born yet.

In this picture, my grandpa is holding the family Bibles. Chief Justice Burger (who was the Chief Justice back then) is administering the oath of office.

The books behind my head are Grandma's opinions and the baby photo on the desk is me!

For a lot of each day, Grandma sits at her desk and reads briefs—long letters from attorneys to the Court—and writes "opinions." Opinions are the written decisions of the Supreme Court. Supreme Court opinions are very important because they explain the Constitution and describe the laws that everyone has to follow.

Grandma has written hundreds of opinions in the years she has been on the Court. She showed me the bound volumes—big books—of all the opinions she has ever written. Grandma sure has a lot of opinions. She also showed me the books that have all the opinions anyone on the Supreme Court has ever written. Those books almost cover the walls in her office.

13

This staircase at the Court winds down four stories. It made me feel a little dizzy when I looked down.

There are even more books in the
Supreme Court library.
Grandma, the other Justices, and their
clerks go to the library to do research
about the law so the Court can decide
cases fairly and correctly. I couldn't
believe how many books
have been written about
the law—and Grandma has
to know as much as she
can about each of them.

Grandma loves music,
and there is a piano in the
Court, too. I played her
some of the Christmas
carols I had been practicing with my
piano teacher. Grandma said that I was
really good and that she wanted me to
keep practicing so that she and Grandpa
could sing along with me when they
come to visit at Christmas.

15

One of my favorite things about

Grandma's job is that she wears really neat robes when she sits on the bench to hear cases. She keeps them in a special locker with her name on it in a little room where Justices get dressed. She let me try them on. My teddy bear even got her very own Supreme Court Justice outfit to wear!

Grandma showed me how to put the robes on. She's been doing it for almost twenty years, so she's a pro!

The ruffle a woman Justice wears around her neck is called a "judicial collar."

Grandma doesn't have to walk around in her robes all the time. When she's not hearing cases, she just wears regular clothes. You wouldn't even know she was a Supreme Court Justice by looking at her.

A cool thing about Grandma

is that she doesn't act like being a Justice is a big deal. When people recognize her in public, she is always nice to them. I think they're a little surprised that she takes the time to talk to them, because they know what an important job she has. Her job is important, but she's also just a grandma like everyone else's grandma.

Besides reading, writing, and deciding cases, Grandma also gives speeches and teaches law students. When I was visiting, some students came to visit from the Sandra Day O'Connor High School in Helotes, Texas. Grandma welcomed them and told them about what it was like to be a Supreme Court Justice. She even wore a varsity letter jacket and wished their athletic team—the Panthers—good luck! She's very proud to have a school named after her.

Doesn't Grandma look proud to be a Panther?

On nice days,

Grandma likes to have lunch in the courtyard with her clerks. It's also a pretty, private place just to sit and relax.

★

Grandma likes to teach

me things, so we went to a lot of interesting places around Washington. One of my favorites was the Roosevelt Memorial. It is a big outdoor museum dedicated to Franklin Delano Roosevelt, our thirty-second President.

There are statues of President Roosevelt and of his wife, Eleanor Roosevelt, who was a very important First Lady. When Grandma was a little girl in school, she met Mrs. Roosevelt and was very inspired by her.

Grandma says that she will always remember the First Lady's strong handshake.

My grandpa didn't die in a war, but all the men and women whose names are on the Memorial did. There are more than 58,000 names there.

I also really liked the Vietnam Memorial

It's a very long wall made out of shiny black granite, and it has inscribed on it the name of every American who died in the Vietnam War. Grandma likes it because she says it's important to honor the people who have served our country, like my grandpa did in the Army.

The National Archives,

where the original Constitution is kept, was another really interesting place to visit. It's dark and cool in the Archives, because the Constitution is more than two hundred years old and could disintegrate if it were exposed to light or heat. The Constitution is four pages long and looks sort of green. It's in handwriting that looks like calligraphy. I was surprised that it wasn't typed, but they didn't have computers for important documents back then.

★

The National Archives building is another beautiful old building full of history. If you visit Washington, D.C., you should check it out.

It's hard to believe

that four pieces of paper could survive for hundreds of years, but there they were! I could read them and everything. There was a long line of people who wanted to see the Constitution. I think everyone knows how important it is to our country and just wants to get a peek at it.

For fun, Grandma and I like to go to the park and museums. A couple of places we really like to visit are the statue of Albert Einstein on Constitution Avenue, and Hains Point, where there is a big sculpture of a giant waking up and stretching out of the ground. Both of the statues are so big that you can climb all over them.

⭐

Above: Grandma says that Albert Einstein was one of the smartest people who ever lived.

The Air and Space Museum is also neat, especially the real spacecraft. Grandma told me that one of the big murals there was painted by an Arizona artist. Since Grandma grew up in Arizona and I still live there, that mural was one of our favorite things.

★ I hope I get to ride in a spacecraft like this one someday!

Grandma and I like to eat pizza and frozen yogurt.

While I was visiting her, we had lunch at the Supreme Court cafeteria, where the pizza is pretty good. We went out for ice cream, too.

Grandma and I both like chocolate ice cream and frozen yogurt best.

★ **For the whole weekend, Grandma made me feel like a princess.**

Of course, we also like to go shopping.

Who doesn't? Grandma likes the bookstore best. I like the toy store. We compromised and went to both.

Even if we don't do anything special, Grandma just likes to spend time with me.

★

Grandma gets to take the summer off,

just like we do at school. She usually comes home to Arizona at the end of June and stays all summer, until around the time I am going back to school.

People ask me a lot whether I want to be a Supreme Court Justice when I grow up. I'm not really sure. There are so many things I like to do: play with my dog, Buffy; write stories; hang out with my sister and brother, Keely and Adam; go shopping with my mom; play the piano. But it would be cool to have my very own Supreme Court Justice robes to wear.

Meanwhile, we have a pageant at school for which we all have to dress up like our favorite heroes or heroines. Grandma says I can borrow her robes for that.

Grandma is **my** heroine.

★

If You Want to Be a Supreme Court Justice . . .

You should also want to be a lawyer or a judge. Although the Constitution does not require it, all Supreme Court Justices are lawyers. Almost all are judges before they become Justices. Sandra Day O'Connor was a judge on the Arizona Court of Appeals.

Study hard in school. To become a lawyer— and later a Justice—you have go to college and then law school. After you graduate from law school, you must take the bar exam in the state where you want to practice law. The bar exam lasts two or three days and tests you on everything you studied in law school.

Be prepared to be patient. Most people are at least 25 years old by the time they become lawyers, and most have practiced law for many years in order to become a judge. Most Supreme Court Justices are in their 40s or 50s before they are appointed by the President.

Be yourself. When Presidents appoint Supreme Court Justices, they consider men and women of all races, religions, lifestyles, and backgrounds. It is important to know that any Justice a President chooses must also be approved by the Senate, which will examine a person's personal life as well as professional qualifications.

Serve an apprenticeship after law school. Many young lawyers are clerks, or helpers, for judges across the country. Clerkships are usually for one year and help lawyers learn more about the law and the court system. All Supreme Court Justices have clerks who help them research the law and write opinions.

Obey the law. To become a lawyer, judge, or Justice, you must follow the law. People who have committed serious crimes are not allowed to become lawyers and cannot be Supreme Court Justices.

Watch lawyers in court. You can watch trials on "Court TV." You can also call lawyers in your community, tell them you are interested in being a lawyer, and ask them if you can watch them in court. Many courts have public information officers who are happy to give you information about when interesting cases are being heard.

Develop strong reading and writing skills. All lawyers, judges, and Justices do a great deal of reading and writing. Some of them consider it to be their primary job!

Stay healthy. Being a Justice is hard but rewarding work! Supreme Court Justices hold their jobs for life, or until they decide to retire. Many Justices continue to serve on the Court until they are in their 70s or 80s.